A GUIDE TO
TRUE
PEACE

A GUIDE TO
TRUE
PEACE

or
A Method Of Attaining To Inward And Spiritual Prayer

Spiritual principles taken primarily from the writings of Francois Fenelon, Madame Jeanne Guyon, and Miguel de Molinos.

Shoals, Indiana

A Guide to True Peace

Published by Kingsley Press
PO Box 973
Shoals, IN 47581
USA
Tel. (800) 971-7985
www.kingsleypress.com
E-mail: sales@kingsleypress.com

ISBN: 978-1-937428-04-4

Contents

Introduction

This devotional classic was originally produced with the intention of nourishing the spiritual life of believers at the dawn of the Industrial Age. Scientific knowledge and human ingenuity were gaining ascendancy in every aspect of society and life. There was a need for a practical guide on what it means to abide in Christ, to live with an active knowledge of the presence of God. Over 180 years later, this book is still entirely relevant.

Our modern "hi-tech" world moves at a pace that allows little time for quiet and stillness before God. A media-controlled society has turned our focus to external things – appearance, image, presentation, and results. The exterior may be glossy, but the interior is often empty and barren.

The principles found in *A Guide To True Peace* deal with the issues of the interior man. They rest upon the fact that those who have devoted their lives to Christ are now the temple of the Holy Spirit; the divine presence of God dwells within them. The remainder of the book deals with what it means to allow that divine Spirit to have His full sway in our lives through denial of self, submission, and obedience. It also considers the blessings of faith and inward prayer, and how the practical results of such a life will lead us into divine union with Almighty God. This union is the place of *true peace*.

This divine union is not some monastic life of mystical passivity, nor is it the "new age" teaching of human divinity within. Rather it is a life of submission to the sovereign will of God. The life of rest and peace is one of activity and spiritual work, but it occurs as we let God act through us. There is no striving when the Holy Spirit is given full control of our lives. We can live in a state of harmony with God and recognise His will and ways in all that is going on within us and around us.

A Guide To True Peace is based largely upon *The Spiritual Guide* by Miguel de Molinos, *A Short Method Of Prayer* by Madame Guyon, and *The Maxims Of The Saints* by Francois Fenelon. These three were the leading figures in the 17th century European spiritual movement known as "Quietism." They acquired this label through the teaching that God is known through the prayer of inward silence when all human thought and feeling is quiet and still.

The Spanish-born Molinos (1626-1697) was the first to put forth this teaching on "inward prayer." The results within the Roman Catholic establishment were enormous. It is estimated that he had up to 20,000 followers in Naples, Italy who were practising this "revolutionary" communion with God. Unwilling to allow personal relationship with God to be preached so freely and successfully, the Jesuits and the Inquisition joined together to stop the flood tide. *A Spiritual Guide* was condemned and Molinos imprisoned in 1685. He remained there until his death in 1697.

At about the same time, Madame Jeanne de la Mothe Guyon (1648-1717) was putting forth similar teachings in France. It seems that she was not familiar with, or even aware of, the growing movement in Italy. She simply saw the emptiness of the Romanist faith at the time and felt the need for a living, vibrant relationship with God for every individual. Her *Short Method Of Prayer* and other writings brought her into direct conflict with the ecclesiastical authorities. She was imprisoned three separate times, including four years in the infamous Bastille. Upon her release in 1702, she was banished for life to Blois, France where she spent her last years. Although in exile, she was visited by religious seekers from near and far. Still holding to her beliefs and practice, she lived her final days as a testimony of submission and devotion to her Lord.

Francois de Salignac de Lamothe Fenelon, Archbishop of Cambrai (1651-1715), was the most notable and fervent of Guyon's French followers. In his earlier days, Fenelon was the private tutor to the grandson of Louis XIV and a regular visitor in the King's Court. However, his religious life and views soon landed him in trouble with those closest to the King, and he was sentenced to internal exile in Cambrai. He would remain there for the rest of his life. It was in Cambrai that he wrote his book, *Maxims Of The Saints*, which was an attempt to defend the teachings regarding inner communion with God. Although Fenelon himself was highly respected for his holiness and purity of life, his writings as to how he attained this way of life were condemned. This book was also banished from print by the Vatican.

All three of these individuals suffered great persecution and loss for the "heresy" that they taught and lived. The Church of Rome tried repeatedly to stamp out this concept of personal union with God. Their writings were condemned and often burned by the hundreds. Yet their teachings and writings are still sought after and valued today, as they have been since their time of pilgrimage here on earth.

Men such as John Wesley, Count Zinzendorf, Hudson Taylor, and Watchman Nee have recommended their works as great sources of spiritual direction and nourishment.

It is with this in mind that we have modernised this classic of devotional life. We believe that in these days of uncertainty and turmoil, it is of great importance that the followers of Jesus Christ know what it means to have personal communion with Him. The principles in this little book, if meditated upon and applied, will be of great help to all who are wholeheartedly seeking more of God.

With regard to the content of the book, it has not been abridged. The message is as it was at the time of original publication. We have simply replaced words that may have developed different meanings, or which are no longer utilised. We have also simplified the sentence and paragraph structure so that the thoughts are easier to follow and comprehend.

We heartily commend the teaching and principles set forth in the following pages, and we pray that they may bring the reader to a place of divine union with God and into a life of true peace.

—*Bruce Garrison*

Preface

It was said by our blessed Redeemer that, "They who worship the Father must worship *Him* in Spirit and in Truth" (John 4:24). Now the object of this work is to explain, in a simple and familiar manner, how this only true worship can be acceptably performed, and how inward, spiritual Prayer can be rightly attained.

Few authors have written with greater clearness on this subject than those from whose works this little volume has been chiefly compiled. They, therefore, have been preferred. At the same time, it has been thought necessary to simplify and render more intelligible some of their terms in order that they may be more generally understood.

While some into whose hands this little treatise may fall will receive it as a Messenger of glad Tidings, there will doubtless be others who may not feel disposed to place much dependence on the simple manner of drawing near to their Creator that is pointed out in these pages.

Let those who think such, however, not judge according to mere appearance, but laying aside all reasoning on the matter, in humility and simplicity, let them actually make an effort to put the principles into practice. They can feel for themselves whether what is stated within will not prove to be something more than an empty dream of the imagination or a cunningly devised fable.

If they do this in sincerity of heart, they will soon have to acknowledge, to their great consolation, that these are indeed substantial, effective, and incontrovertible Truths. They will clearly see that this is the true way to become purified from our many defilements, to be instructed in heavenly mysteries, to taste of the wine of the kingdom, and to partake of that bread of life which nourishes us up unto everlasting life.

1

The Spirit Of God Dwells In The Heart Of Man

It is certain from Scripture that the Spirit of God dwells within us, that a "manifestation of the Spirit is given for the common good" (1 Corinthians 12:7), and that this is "the true Light which enlightens every man" (John 1:9). This is the "grace of God that brings salvation and which has appeared to all men. It teaches us to say `No' to ungodliness and worldly passions, and to live self-controlled, upright, and godly lives in this present age" (Titus 2:11-12).

But we take too little notice of this internal Teacher which is the soul of our soul, and by which we are able to form good thoughts and desires. God does not cease to reprove us for evil and to influence us toward that which is good, but the noise of the outside world, and our own inner passions, deafens us and hinders us from hearing Him.

We must retire from all outward objects and silence all the desires and wandering imaginations of the mind, that in this profound silence of the whole soul we may heed the inexpressible voice of the Divine Teacher. We must listen with an attentive ear, for it is a still small voice. It is not indeed a voice uttered in words as when a man speaks to his friend. Instead, it is an inner perception infused by the secret operations and influences of the Divine Spirit, insinuating to us obedience, patience, meekness, humility, and all the other Christian virtues in a language perfectly intelligible to the attentive soul.

But how seldom is it that the soul keeps itself silent enough for God to speak! The murmurs of our vain desires, and of our self-love, disturb all the teachings of the Divine Spirit. Ought we then to be surprised if so many persons – apparently devout, but in reality too full of their own wisdom and confidence in their own virtues – are not able to hear it, and that they look upon this internal Word as the idle fancy of fanatics? Alas! What is it they aim at with their vain reasoning? The external word, even of the Gospel, would be but an empty sound without this living and fruitful Word in the interior, to interpret and open it to the understanding.

Jesus Christ says: "Behold, I stand at the door and knock. If anyone hears my voice and opens the door, I will come in and eat with him, and he with me" (Revelation 3:20). His knocks are the stirrings of His Spirit that touches us and operates in us. And to respond to these stirrings and follow them is to open up to Him.

God speaks to impenitent sinners, but these, engrossed in the eager pursuit of worldly pleasures and the gratification of their evil passions, are not able to hear Him. His Word to them passes for a fable. But woe unto those who receive their consolation in this life. The time will come when their vain joys shall be astonished with terror.

He speaks to sinners who are in the path of conversion. These persons feel the remorses of their conscience, and these remorses are the voice of God that reproves them inwardly of their vices. When they are truly touched, they have no difficulty comprehending this secret voice, for it is this that so pierces them to the heart. It is that two-edged sword within them which goes even to the dividing of the soul from itself: "For the word of God is living and active. Sharper than any double-edged sword, it penetrates even to dividing soul and spirit, joints and marrow; it judges the thoughts and attitudes of the heart" (Hebrews 4:12).

He speaks to persons who are enlightened and learned, and whose life from the outside seems quite regular and adorned with many virtues. But often these persons, full of themselves and of their knowledge, give so much effort to hearing themselves that they are unable to listen to God. God, who seeks only to communicate Himself, finds no place (so to speak) where He can introduce Himself into these souls that are so full of themselves and so overfed with their own wisdom and virtues.

He hides His secrets from the wise and prudent and reveals them to the low and simple. Our blessed Redeemer said, "I praise you, Father, Lord of heaven and earth, because you have hidden these things from the wise and learned, and revealed them to little children" (Matthew

11:25). He delights to dwell with the humble and child-like and to disclose to them His unutterable secrets.

It is these who are more peculiarly qualified for receiving in a greater measure the gift of faith. Being willing that the pride of Reason should be laid in the dust, they do not obstruct the entrance of this gift of the Holy Spirit by their vain arguments. Rather, they believe with simplicity and confidence.

2

On Faith

There are two sorts or degrees of Faith. The first is that by which the mind gives its assent to the truth of a thing on the testimony of another. The second is of a more exalted nature, being of Divine origin, and is a gift of the Holy Spirit. By the first, we believe in the existence of God and in the truths that He has revealed to us in the Holy Scriptures.

It is an essential principle in the beginning of the spiritual path, because "he that comes to God must believe that He exists and that He rewards those who earnestly seek Him" (Hebrews 11:6). And if we put our whole trust in Him and endeavour in all things to obey Him, we shall be in a state of preparation for the reception for that true and living Faith which is "the gift of God" (Ephesians 2:8).

It is only by this Faith that we shall be enabled to overcome all our spiritual enemies and to clearly understand those mysteries which are incomprehensible to human reason, for reason, being born of man, is weak and uncertain and easily errs. But faith, being born of God, cannot err. Reason, therefore, must follow and submit to faith; it must not go before and control it.

It is by Faith that "being justified, we have peace with God through our Lord Jesus Christ" (Romans 5:1). And when this precious gift has been granted to us, it produces in us Hope (Romans 5:2), Love (1 Peter 1:8), Confidence (Ephesians 3:12), Joy (Romans 5:2), and Holiness of heart (Acts 15:9).

We shall then be enabled to feel an entire dependence on the goodness, power, justice, and mercy of God, and a confidence in His promises. We will also more fully experience and comprehend the operations of His Spirit on the mind.

Faith is an essential requirement for the proper performance of all our duties to God. Indeed, without it we cannot possibly please Him (Hebrews 11:6), neither should we ever be able to seek Him or believe in the influence of His Holy Spirit upon our souls.

It is by Faith that we are supported on our pathway to Peace. By Faith we are enabled to persevere through the difficulties and attacks which we may have to encounter on our way. It is through this holy principle that we suffer the pains of dryness and lack of consolation without fainting. For by it we are strengthened to "endure as seeing Him who is invisible" (Hebrews 11:27). And it is only by Faith that we can attain to the practice of true, inward, and spiritual prayer.

3

On Prayer

Prayer is an intercourse of the soul with God. It is not a work of the head but of the heart, and it ought always to continue. It is the medium through which life and food are conveyed to the soul and the channel through which the gifts and graces of the Holy Spirit flow and are communicated. Every secret aspiration of the soul to God is prayer. All are therefore capable of prayer, and all are called to it, just as all are called to and are capable of salvation.

The apostle Paul has encouraged us to "pray without ceasing" (1 Thessalonians 5:17). Our Lord said: "I say to you all, watch and pray" (Mark 13:33,37; 15:38).

Come then, all you that are thirsty, to these living waters (Revelation 22:17). Do not lose your precious moments in "digging out cisterns that will hold no water" (Jeremiah 2:13). Come, you hungering souls who can find nothing upon which to feed; come, and you will be fully satisfied. Come you poor afflicted ones who groan beneath your load of wretchedness and pain, and you shall find ease and comfort. Come, you who are sick, to your Physician and do not be afraid to approach Him because you are filled with diseases. Expose them to His view, and they shall be healed.

Children, draw near to your Father, and He will embrace you in the arms of Love. Come, you poor, stray, wandering sheep, return to your Shepherd. Come, you who have been seeking happiness in worldly pleasures and pursuits, but have failed to find in them the satisfaction that you expected. Come and learn how to be truly happy here and eternally happy hereafter. Come, sinners, to your Saviour. Come, you who are dull, ignorant, or illiterate – you who think that you are the most incapable of prayer – for you are peculiarly called and adapted to prayer. Let all without exception come, for Jesus Christ has called all.

You must however learn a manner of prayer that may be exercised at all times and will not interrupt outward activities. It may be equally practised by all ranks and conditions of men – by the poor as well as the rich, by the illiterate as well as the learned. It cannot, therefore, be a prayer of the head but of the heart. It is a manner of prayer that nothing can interrupt but irregular and disordered affections. And though you may think yourselves too ignorant for heavenly attainments, yet, by prayer the possession and enjoyment of God is easily obtained. He has a greater desire to give Himself to us than we have to receive Him.

Prayer is the guide to perfection and the sovereign good. It delivers us from every vice and obtains for us every virtue, because the one great means to becoming perfect is to walk in the presence of God. He Himself has said, "Walk in my presence and be perfect" (Genesis 17:1). It is only by prayer that we are brought into, and maintained in, His presence. Once we have fully known Him and the sweetness of His love, we shall find it impossible to relish anything so much as Himself.

4

All Are Capable Of Attaining To Inward And Spiritual Prayer

If all were eager to pursue the spiritual path, shepherds, while they watched their flocks, might have the Spirit of the early Christians, and the farmer at the plough would maintain a blessed communion with His God. The manufacturer, while he exhausted his outward man with labour, would be renewed in internal strength. Every form of sin and vice would shortly disappear, and all mankind would become true followers of the Good Shepherd.

Oh, once the heart is submitted, how easily all moral evil is corrected! It is for this reason that God, above all things, requires the heart. It is the conquest of the heart alone that can fully destroy those dreadful vices – drunkenness, blasphemy, immorality, envy, and theft – which are so predominant among men. If He gained full control of the hearts of all, then Jesus Christ would become the universal and peaceful Sovereign, and all mankind would be wholly renewed.

The decay of internal holiness is unquestionably the source of the various problems that have arisen in the world. All of these would be corrected or overthrown if inward religion were to be established. If, instead of engaging those who are wandering in vain disputes, we could but teach them to simply believe and diligently to pray, we would lead them sweetly to God.

Oh how inexpressibly great is the loss sustained by mankind from the neglect of the interior life!

Some excuse themselves by saying that this is a dangerous way. They argue that simple people are unable to comprehend spiritual matters. But the Oracles of Truth affirm the contrary. And where is the danger of walking in the only true way (John 14:6), which is Jesus

Christ? What is the danger of giving ourselves up to Him, fixing our eyes continually on Him, placing all our confidence in His grace, and turning with all the strength of our soul to His pure Love?

The simple, so far from being incapable of this perfection, are by their teachability, innocence, and humility, peculiarly adapted and qualified for its attainment. As they are not accustomed to reasoning, they are less concerned with speculations and less tenacious in defending their own opinions. Even from their want of learning, they submit more freely to the teachings of the Divine Spirit; whereas others, who are blinded by self-sufficiency and enslaved by prejudice, give great resistance to the operations of Grace.

We are told in Scripture that God gives understanding to the simple (Psalm 119:130), and we are also assured that God cares for them: "The Lord preserves the simple" (Psalm 116:6). Christ said to His apostles: "Let the little children come to me ... for the kingdom of heaven belongs to such as these" (Matthew 19:14).

The simple are incapable of reasoning; teach them, therefore, the prayer of the heart and not of the head – the prayer of God's Spirit and not of man's invention.

Alas! By wanting them to pray in elaborate forms, and by being curiously critical of their prayers, you create their chief obstacles. The children have been led astray from the best of Fathers by your endeavouring to teach them too refined and too polished a language.

The simple and undisguised emotions of brotherly love are infinitely more expressive than the most studied language. The Spirit of God needs none of our arrangements and methods. When it pleases Him, He turns shepherds into prophets. And instead of excluding any from the Temple of Prayer, He throws the gates open wide so that all may enter in. Wisdom cries out: "Let all who are simple come in here!" she says to those who lack judgment. "Come, eat my food and drink the wine I have mixed" (Proverbs 9:3-5).

To teach man to seek God in his heart, to think of Him, to return to Him whenever he finds he has wandered from Him, and to do and suffer all things with the single purpose of pleasing Him is the natural and ready process. It is leading the soul to the very source of Grace, where all that is necessary for sanctification is to be found.

Oh that all would immediately put themselves into this way – which is Jesus Christ – that His kingdom might be established in their hearts! For as it is the heart alone that can oppose His sovereignty, so it is by the subjection of the heart that His sovereignty is most highly exalted.

Since none can attain this blessed state except those whom God Himself leads and places in it, we do not pretend to introduce any into it but only to point out the shortest and safest road that leads to it. We encourage you not to be slowed down in your progress by any external exercises and not to rest in the shadow instead of the substance.

If the water of eternal life is shown to some thirsty souls, how inexpressibly cruel it would be, by confining them to a method of external forms and orders, to prevent their reaching it so that their longing is never satisfied and they perish with thirst!

Oh you blind and foolish men who pride yourselves on science, wisdom, wit, and power! How well do you prove the truth of what God has said – that His secrets are hidden from the wise and prudent, and they are revealed unto *The Little Ones – The Babes!* (Matthew 11:25).

5

Method Of Attaining To True Prayer

The sort of prayer to which we have alluded is inward silence. Here the soul, disengaged from all outward things, in holy stillness, humble reverence, and lively faith, waits patiently to feel the Divine Presence and to receive the precious influences of the Holy Spirit.

When you retire for this purpose, which should be your frequent practice, you should consider yourself as being placed in the presence of God, looking with a single eye to Him, resigning yourself entirely into His hands to receive from Him whatsoever He may be pleased to give you. At the same time, you calmly endeavour to fix your mind in peace and silence, quitting all your own reasonings and not willingly thinking on anything, no matter how good or how profitable it may appear to be. Should any vain imaginations present themselves, you should gently turn from them; thus faithfully and patiently you wait to feel the Divine Presence.

If while you are thus engaged, something of inward stillness or a degree of the softening influence of the Divine Spirit is mercifully granted you, you should prize these manifestations of the Presence of God in your soul and be carefully and reverently attentive to them.

Be cautious however not to endeavour to increase them by your own activity, for by so doing, you will draw the mind off from that state of holy stillness and humble watchfulness which you should be desirous as much as possible to maintain. By fanning the flame there is a danger of extinguishing it and thus depriving the soul of that nourishment which was intended for it.

A lively sense of the Presence of God will extricate us speedily from numberless mental wanderings, remove us far from external objects, and bring us near unto our God who is only to be found in our inmost centre – the Temple in which He dwells (1 Corinthians 6:19). When we are thus fully turned inward and warmly penetrated with a sense of His Presence, we should in stillness and repose, with reverence, confidence, and love, allow the blessed food of which we have tasted to sink deep into the soul.

The prayer of inward silence is the easiest and most profitable path. With a simple view or attention to God, the soul becomes like a humble supplicant before its Lord, or as a child that casts itself into the safe bosom of its mother. It is also the most secure, because it is removed from the operations of the imagination. The imagination, being always exposed to the delusions of the enemy, is often beguiled into extravagances or extremes and is easily bewildered and deceived. This causes the soul to be deprived of its peace.

It will at first be difficult, from the habit the mind will have acquired of being always away from home, roving here and there and from subject to subject, to restrain it and free it from those wanderings which are an impediment to prayer.

Indeed those wanderings of the imagination, with which beginners are for some time tried, are permitted in order to prove their faith, exercise their patience, and to show them how little they can do in their own strength. The wanderings also teach them to depend upon God alone for strength to overcome all their difficulties – for "by his own strength shall no man prevail" (1 Samuel 2:9). If they place all their hope in Him and faithfully persevere, every obstacle will be gradually removed, and they will find that they will be enabled to approach Him with ease. The inward silence will not only be attended with much less difficulty, but at times will be found to be easy, sweet, and delightful. They will know that this is the true way of finding God and feel "His name to be as ointment poured forth" (Song of Songs 1:3).

Although we should at all times be very watchful and diligent in recalling our wandering thoughts, restraining them as much as we can in due subjection, still, a direct contest with them only serves to augment and irritate them. However, by calling to mind that we are in the presence of God and endeavouring to sink down under a sense and perception of His presence by simply turning inwards, we wage unknowingly a very advantageous, though indirect, war against them.

Those who have not learned to read are not, on that account, excluded from prayer, for the great Teacher who teaches all things is Jesus Christ Himself (John 14:26). They should learn this fundamental rule: that "the Kingdom of God is within them" (Luke 17:21). It is there only – within – that it must be sought.

"The Kingdom of God is within you," said our blessed Redeemer. Abandon, therefore, the cares and pleasures of this wretched world and turn to the Lord with all your heart, and your soul shall find rest (Matthew 11:28-29). If you withdraw your attention from outward things and keep it fixed on the internal Teacher, endeavouring to obey Him in whatever He may require of you, you will soon perceive the coming of the kingdom of God (Matthew 6:10). This kingdom of God is that "righteousness, peace and joy in the Holy Ghost" (Romans 14:17) which cannot be received by sensual and worldly men.

It is for want of inward retirement and prayer that our lives are so imperfect, and that we are neither penetrated nor warmed with the divine Light of Truth, Christ the Light (John 1:9). We should, therefore, be in the daily practice of it. There is nobody who is so occupied that they are not able to find a few moments of inward retirement with God.

The less we practise silent prayer, the less desire we have for it. Our minds become set upon outward things, and we contract at last such a habit that it is very hard to turn them inward.

"The Lord is in His Holy Temple, let all the earth keep silence before Him" (Habakkuk 2:20). The silence of all our earthly thoughts and desires is absolutely indispensable if we would hear the secret voice of the Divine Instructor. Hearing is a sense formed to receive sounds; it is rather passive than active, an admitting but not communicating sensation.

If we would hear, we must lend the ear for that purpose. Therefore, Christ, *The eternal Word* (Revelation 19:13) – without whose divine voice the soul is dead, dark, and barren – when He would speak with us, requires the most silent attention to His all-quickening and effective voice.

We should forget ourselves and all self-interest and listen and be attentive to the voice of our God. Outward silence is absolutely necessary for the cultivation and improvement of inward silence. Indeed, it is impossible that we should become truly internal without the love and practice of outward silence and solitude. Unquestionably, our being internally engaged with God is wholly incompatible with being busy and employed in the numerous trifles that surround us.

When, through foolishness or unfaithfulness, we become given to foolish or harmful pleasures, or as it were uncentred, it is of immediate importance to gently and peacefully turn inward once again. In this way we learn to preserve the spirit and unction of prayer throughout the day; for if the prayer of inward silence were wholly confined to any appointed half-hour or hour, we would reap but little fruit.

It is of the greatest importance for the soul to go to prayer with confidence and a pure and selfless love that seeks nothing from God but the ability to please Him and to do His will. A servant who is diligent only in proportion to his hope of reward renders himself unworthy of all reward. Go then to prayer, not that you enjoy spiritual delights but that you may be full or empty, just as it pleases God. This will preserve you in an evenness of spirit, either in desertion or in consolation, and will prevent your being surprised at dryness or the apparent repulses of God.

Constant prayer is to keep the heart always right toward God. Strive then, when you come to prayer, not to allow your mind to be too entangled with outward things. Rather, endeavour to be totally resigned to the Divine Will that God may do with you and yours according to His heavenly pleasure. Rely on Him as on a kind and loving Father.

Though you may be taken up with your outward affairs, and your mind prevented from being actually fixed on Him, even then you will always carry a fire around in you that will never go out. On the contrary, it will nourish a secret prayer that will be like a lamp continually lighted before the throne of God.

A son who loves his Father does not always think distinctly of him. Many objects draw away his mind, but these never interrupt filial love. Whenever his Father returns into his thoughts, he loves Him, and he feels in the very depths of his heart that he has never stopped loving Him for one moment, though he has ceased to think of Him. We should love our heavenly Father in this manner. It is by true religion alone that we are enabled to call God our Father, and that we can indeed become His sons.

True religion is a heaven-born thing. It is an emanation of the Truth and Goodness of God upon the spirits of men, whereby they are formed into a similitude and likeness of Himself and become "partakers of the Divine Nature" (2 Peter 1:4). A true Christian is in every way of a most noble extraction, of a heavenly and divine pedigree, being born, as John expresses it, "from above" (John 3:3). In another place he says: "Behold what manner of love the Father has given unto us, that we should be called the sons of God!" (1 John 3:1).

If considerations such as these are not sufficient to convince us of the folly of our attachment to perishing things and to stimulate us to press after those which obtain for us such great and glorious privileges, we must indeed be sunk into a state of deep and deplorable insensibility. From such a condition it would be impossible to arouse us, even "if one were to rise from the dead" (Luke 16:31).

NOTE: If you wish to receive real profit from the Holy Scriptures and other spiritual books, you must peruse them with deep attention and introversion of mind. Have the intention, no matter what you have chosen to read, of reading only a small part of it. Endeavour to taste and digest it, to extract the essence and substance of the material. Proceed no further while any savour or relish remains in a passage. When this subsides, take up your book again and proceed as before, seldom reading more than half a page at a time. It is not the quantity that is read, but the manner of reading that yields us profit. Those who read fast reap no more advantage than a bee would do by only skimming over the surface of a flower, instead of waiting to penetrate into it and extract its sweets. If this method were pursued, we would be more fully prepared for solitude and prayer. (Madame Guyon)

6

On Spiritual Dryness

No sooner will you have given yourself up to serve the Lord in this inward way than He will begin to purify you and try your faith in order to draw you nearer to Himself. For this purpose, He will lead you through the paths of dryness and desertion.

When you endeavour to fix your mind in silence in order to feel after your God, you will not experience the comfort and refreshment you expected. On the contrary, you will be beset with a multitude of troublesome and importunate imaginations – even more than usual. These will be so many that you will begin to think that you labour to no purpose and that the prayer of internal silence is an attainment to which you need not aspire, seeing that your imagination is so ungovernable and your mind so void of good. But this state of dryness is very profitable if it be suffered with patience.

The Lord makes use of the veil of dryness so that we are not always aware of what He is working in us; this keeps us humble. If we felt and knew what He was working in our souls, satisfaction and presumption would get in. We would imagine that we were doing some good thing and reckon ourselves as very near to God. This self-complacency would prevent our spiritual advancement.

Even though in the prayer of mental stillness you may feel yourself to be in a dry and comfortless state – not being able to get rid of your troublesome thoughts, nor experience any light, consolation, or spiritual feeling – do not be discouraged nor desist from your undertaking. Resign yourself at that time with vigour and patiently persevere as in His presence. While you persevere in that manner, your soul will be internally improved.

Do you believe that when you come from prayer in the same manner as you began it, without feeling any profit in yourself, that you have been working in vain? That is a fallacy, because true prayer consists not in enjoying the light and having knowledge of spiritual things, but in enduring with patience and persevering in faith and silence. You continue believing that you are in the Lord's presence, turning your heart to Him with tranquillity and simplicity of mind.

We must be aware that nature is always an enemy to the spirit. When she is deprived of sensible pleasures, she remains weak, melancholy, and full of irritation. Hence from the uneasiness of thoughts, the weariness of body, troublesome sleep, and your inability to curb the senses – every one of which would follow its own pleasure – you will often feel impatient to be at the end of your prayer. Happy are you if you can persevere in the midst of the painful trial! Remember that "they who wait upon the Lord shall renew their strength; they shall mount up with wings as eagles; they shall run and not be weary; they shall walk and not faint" (Isaiah 40:31).

The prayer of internal silence may be well typified by that wrestling which the Holy Scriptures say the patriarch Jacob had all night with God, until the day broke and He blessed him. The soul is to persevere and wrestle with the difficulties that it will meet with in inward prayer without desisting until the Sun of internal Light begins to appear, and the Lord gives it His blessing.

If you go to prayer with the spirit and intention of praying, so long as you do not retract that intention, even though, through misery and frailty, your thoughts may wander, you will nevertheless pray in spirit and in truth.

God, in His own due time, will help you to overcome all your difficulties. When you are least expecting it, He will give you holy purposes and more effectual desire to serve Him. Therefore, do not distrust Him, but only yourself. Remember that, as the apostle says, "He is the Father of mercies and the God of all comfort" (2 Corinthians 1:3). His comforts are sometimes withdrawn, but His mercy endures forever. In His grace, He has deprived you of what was sweet and sensory, because you needed to be humbled.

Be of good courage then. Though it may seem to you that you toil without gaining much, you must remember that we plough and sow before we can reap. If you persevere in faith and patience, you will reap an abundant reward for all your labours.

Would you be so unreasonable as to expect to find without seeking, or for it to be opened to you without your taking the pains to knock? The farmer might as well expect to see his fields waving with grain without his having gone to trouble to put the seed into the ground.

It is no hard matter to stay near to God while you are enjoying His comforts and consolations, but if you would prove your devotion to Him, you must be willing to follow Him through the paths of dryness and desertion. The truth of a friend is not known while he is receiving favours and benefits from us. But if he remains faithful to us when we treat him with coldness and neglect, it will be a proof of the sincerity of his attachment.

Though God has no desire other than to impart Himself to those that love and seek Him, yet He frequently conceals Himself from us so that we may be roused from sloth and induced to seek Him with faithfulness and love. But with what abundant goodness does He reward our faithfulness! How sweetly are these apparent withdrawings of Himself succeeded by the consolations of His love!

David said, "I waited patiently for the Lord; He turned to me and heard my cry. He lifted me out of the slimy pit, out of the mud and mire; He set my feet on a rock and gave me a firm place to stand. He put a new song in my mouth, a hymn of praise to our God" (Psalm 40:1-3).

In seasons of the withdrawal of His Presence, we are apt to believe that it will be a proof of our fidelity and show the fervour of our love if we seek Him by an exertion of our own strength and activity. We also believe this exertion will induce Him to return more speedily. However, this is not the right procedure when we are in such a state.

With patient resignation, with self-abasement, with the reiterated breathings of an ardent but peaceful affection, and with reverential silence, we must wait the return of our beloved. In this way we will demonstrate that we seek nothing but Him and His good pleasure – and not the selfish delights of our own sensations.

It is very common for us, when we feel the sweetness of the grace of God, to believe that we love Him, but it is only in the withdrawings of His Presence that our love can be tried and the measure of it be known. It is during these seasons that we are convinced of the weakness and misery of our nature and how, of ourselves, we are incapable of thinking or doing any good.

There are many who, when they experience the meltings of the heart, shedding of tears, and other sensible delights, think that they are the favourites of God and that at that moment they truly possess Him. However, they then pass all their lives in seeking after those pleasurable sensations.

Such people should be cautious lest they deceive themselves, for these sensible consolations, when they proceed from nature and are caused by their own reflections or self-admiration, hinder them from discerning the true light or making one step towards perfection.

You should therefore be careful to distinguish those mere meltings of the affections from the pure operations that proceed directly from God. Always leave yourselves to be led forward by Him who will be your light in the midst of darkness and dryness.

It is of no small advantage in prayer to patiently suffer the lack of consolation or the persistent trouble of a wandering imagination. When you persevere in these things, it is like offering up one's self in a whole burnt offering and sacrifice. As many times as you make the effort to calmly reject your vain thoughts and peacefully endure your dark and desolate state, so many crowns will the Lord set upon your head.

It is of great importance that you endeavour, at all times, to keep your heart in peace so that you may keep pure the temple of God. The way to keep it in peace is to enter into it by means of inward silence.

When you see yourself more sharply assaulted, retreat into that region of peace. There you will find a fortress that will enable you to triumph over all your enemies, visible and invisible, and over all their snares and temptations. Within this temple resides Divine Aid and Sovereign Rest. Retreat within it, and all will be quiet, secure, peaceful, and calm.

By means of this mental silence, which can only be attained by Divine Help, you may look for tranquillity in tumult, solitude in company, light in darkness, forgetfulness in pressures, vigour in despondency, courage in fear, resistance in temptation, peace in war, and quiet in tribulation.

7

On Defects And Infirmities

If we should get so far off our guard as to again turn to external things in search of happiness, or sink into sinful indulgence, or commit a fault, we must instantly turn inwards. If we have, in such a manner, departed from our God, we should as soon as possible return to Him and patiently endure whatever sensations He is pleased to impress upon us. For He has declared, "Those whom I love I rebuke and discipline" (Revelation 3:19).

When we have committed some fault, it is of great importance to guard against irritation and anxiety, which spring from a secret root of pride and a love of our own excellence. We are hurt by seeing what we truly are, and if we discourage ourselves or grow despondent, we are even more weakened. From our reflections upon the sin, a deep disappointment arises which is often worse than the fault itself.

The truly humble soul is not surprised at its defects or failings. The more miserable and wretched it recognises itself to be, the more it abandons itself to God and presses for a nearer and more intimate union with Him, that it may avail itself of an eternal strength. We should be more inclined to act in this manner, because God Himself has said, "I will instruct you and teach you in the way you should go; I will counsel and watch over you" (Psalm 32:8).

8

On Temptations And Tribulations

We are by nature so sinful, proud, and ambitious, so full of our own appetites, our own judgments and opinions, that if temptations and tribulations were not permitted to test, humble, and purify us, we would never arrive at a state of maturity before God.

The Lord, seeing our misery and perverse inclinations, and being moved to compassion, withdraws His strength from us so we may feel our own weakness. He allows us to be assaulted by violent and painful suggestions of impatience and pride, and numerous other temptations. He causes others, who have long been in the practice of sin – by gluttony, greed, rage, swearing, despair, and a great many other failings – to see their sinful nature, in order that they may know themselves and be humble. With these temptations and dealings, Infinite Goodness humbles our pride, giving us, in them, the most wholesome medicine.

"All our righteousness," says Isaiah, "is as filthy rags" (Isaiah 64:6), through the vanity, conceit, and self-love with which they are defiled. It is, therefore, necessary that they should be purified with the fire of temptation and trial, so that they may be clean, pure, perfect, and complete in the sight of God (James 1:2-4).

The Lord polishes the soul that He draws to Himself with the rough file of temptation, freeing it thereby from the rust of many evil passions and inclinations. By means of temptation and tribulation, He humbles, subjects, and exercises it, showing it its own weakness and misery. In this way He purifies and strips the heart in order that all its operations may be pure and of inestimable value.

Oh, how happy would you be if you could quietly believe that all the trials and temptations by which you are assaulted are permitted for your gain and spiritual profit! But you will perhaps say that when you are bothered by others, or wronged and injured by your neighbour, that this cannot be for your spiritual advantage since it is the effect of their faults and malice.

This is nothing more than a cunning and hidden device of the enemy, because God does not will the sin of another, yet He wills His own effect in you. The trouble that comes to you from another's fault should improve you by increasing your patience and exercising your forbearance and love.

Consider how the Lord makes use of the faults of others for the good of your soul. Oh the greatness of the divine wisdom! Who can pry into the depths of the secret and extraordinary means and the hidden ways by which He guides the soul that He desires to purge, transform, and dignify.

It is often the greatest temptation to be without temptation, because we are then most liable to fall into a state of lukewarmness. Therefore we ought not to fret when it assaults us, but with resignation, peace, and constancy, shut our hearts against it.

If you desire to serve God and arrive at the sublime region of internal peace, you must pass through this rugged path of temptation and tribulation. In this, you will become polished, purged, renewed, and purified.

A direct contest and struggle with temptations only serves to increase them. This withdraws the soul from that adherence to God which should always be its principal occupation to strive after and maintain. The surest and safest method of conquest is simply to turn away from the evil and draw yet nearer and closer to our God.

A little child, on perceiving a monster, does not wait to fight with it, and will scarcely turn its eyes toward it, but quickly shrinks into the bosom of its mother in total confidence of safety. Likewise should the soul turn from the dangers of temptation to its God.

"God is in the midst of her," says the Psalmist, "she shall not be moved; God will help her at break of day" (Psalm 46:5). "The name of the Lord is a strong tower; the righteous run to it and are safe" (Proverbs 18:10).

If we do anything else, and in our weakness attempt to attack our enemies, we shall frequently feel ourselves wounded if not totally defeated. However, by casting ourselves into the presence of God and relying solely on Him, we shall find supplies of strength for our support.

This was the help sought by David: "I have set," he says, "the Lord always before me Because He is at my right hand, I will not be shaken. Therefore my heart is glad and my tongue rejoices; my body will also rest secure" (Psalm 16:8-9). And it is said in Exodus, "The Lord will fight for you; you need only to be still" (14:14).

Although "God cannot be tempted by evil, nor does He tempt anyone" (James 1:13), yet it is evident that temptations are permitted for our good. If rightly endured, they contribute to our refinement. "Therefore consider it pure joy, my brothers, whenever you face trials of many kinds, because you know that the testing of your faith develops perseverance" (James 1:2).

Whenever we are besieged – however painful it may feel to us, or of whatever nature it may be – we should remember that it is said, "Blessed is the man who endures temptation, because when he has stood the test, he will receive the crown of life that God has promised to those who love Him" (James 1:12).

You cannot be hurt by men or devils if you always stay near to God. "Who is going to harm you if you are eager to do good?" (1 Peter 3:13). But if you are hurt, it is your pride, your passions, and your many unsubdued evil tendencies that rise up and injure you. As long as these remain, the enemy will make use of them and seek to draw your mind away from its adherence to God.

"Every man is tempted when he is drawn away by his own lust and enticed" (James 1:14). Therefore know your own corrupt state and the need you have to be purified by temptation. Always stay alert for fear that the tireless enemy should gain access to your soul by his insinuations and pleasing allurements.

In your passage through life, there are many things that he will offer as temptations, and he will suit these to your present situation and condition. He is always endeavouring to produce in you an inordinate inclination and desire for these things. And if you give way to them while you are tempted in this way, there will be great danger of your being entirely overcome.

If the malicious enemy is not resisted in his first attack, he enters by gradual advances and takes entire possession of the heart. As long as our opposition to him is delayed by habitual negligence, our power to oppose becomes lesser every day, and the strength of the adversary proportionately greater.

Therefore when you feel a strong and eager desire for anything whatever, and you find your inclinations carrying you much too strongly to act upon it, strive to moderate yourself by retreating inwardly and seeking after tranquillity of mind. To do all things well, we must do them as in the presence of God. Otherwise we will soon lose sight of our correct centre, and we will be in danger of being completely overthrown.

Oh blessed soul! If you would be content and quiet in the fire of temptation and tribulation, and allow yourself to be fully tested and tried by patiently enduring the assaults of the enemy and the desertion of heavenly good, how soon you would find yourself rich in celestial treasures! How soon the Divine bounty would make a rich throne in your soul and a glorious habitation in which you could refresh and comfort yourself!

You must know that although the Lord may temporarily *visit*, yet He makes His *home* in none but peaceful souls, and those in whom the fire of temptation and trial has consumed *all* their corrupt inclinations. The Lord does not come to rest just anywhere, but where quietness reigns and self-love is banished.

If from chaos His omnipotence has produced so many wonders in the creation of the world, what will He not be able to do in your own soul – created in His own image and likeness – if you keep constant, quiet, and resigned, with a true sense of your own nothingness?

"Do not throw away your confidence, which will be richly rewarded" (Hebrews 10:35), but remain constant. O blessed soul! Remain constant, for it will not be as you imagine. Not at any time are you nearer to God than in such times of desertion and trial of your faith. Although the sun is hidden in the clouds, it does not change its place nor lose any degree of its brightness.

The Lord permits these painful temptations and desertions to purge and polish you, to cleanse and disrobe you of self. His purpose is that through these trials you may become entirely His and give yourself up wholly to serve Him.

Oh how much there is to be purified in a soul that desires to arrive at the holy mountain of perfection and of transformation with God! While any portion of evil, any thing of self, remains in us, we must be subject to temptation. When self is annihilated, there is then nothing left for the tempter to act upon. Oh how resigned, naked, denied, annihilated, ought the soul to be if it would not hinder the entrance of the Divine Lord nor His continual communion with it!

9

On Self-Denial

He who expects to arrive at a place of perfect union of the soul with God, by means of spiritual ease and comfort, will find himself mistaken. From the depravity of our nature, we must expect to suffer and be in some measure purified before we can be in any degree fit for a union with God, or permitted to taste of the joy of His Presence.

Be patient, therefore, under all the sufferings which God is pleased to send you. If your love for Him is pure, you will not seek Him less in suffering than in ease. Surely He should be as much loved in *that* as in *this*, since it was by suffering on the cross that He made the greater display of His own love for you.

Do not be like those who give themselves to Him at one season and withdraw from Him at another. They give themselves only to be caressed, but they pull themselves back again when they come to be crucified. If they do not completely pull back, they at least turn to the world for comfort and consolation.

You will not find full comfort in anything but a free and full surrender of your will to the Divine Will. He who savours not the cross savours not the things that are of God (Matthew 16:23), but a heart that savours the Cross finds the bitterest things to be sweet. "To the hungry even what is bitter tastes sweet" (Proverbs 27:7). God gives the Cross, and the Cross gives us God.

We may be assured that there is an internal advance wherever there is an advance in the way of the Cross.

As soon as anything presents itself as a suffering and you feel repugnance against it, resign yourself immediately to God with respect to the situation, giving yourself up to Him in sacrifice. You will find that when the Cross arrives it will not be so very burdensome, because you had already disposed yourself to a willing reception of it. Jesus Christ Himself was willing to suffer its utmost rigours. We often bear the cross in weakness, and at other times in strength; all should be equal to us in the will of God.

If any other way but bearing the cross and dying to his own will could have led man from that fallen and corrupt state, which he is in by nature, Christ would have taught it and established it by His own example. But He has required the bearing of the cross of all who desire to follow Him. He has said to all, without exception, "If any man will come after me, let him deny himself, take up his cross, and follow me" (Matthew 16:24). Why then do you fear to take up the cross that will direct you to the path that leads to the kingdom of God?

From the cross is derived heavenly meekness, true fortitude, the joys of the spirit, the conquest of self, the perfection of holiness! There is no freedom, no hope of the continuation of the divine life in us, except by our taking up the cross to put to death our carnal appetites and inclinations. Resurrection life comes through the death of self, and there is no means to obtain this life and peace but by dying to the corruption of our fallen nature!

Take up your cross therefore and follow Jesus in the path that leads to everlasting peace. He has gone ahead, bearing that cross upon which He died for you, that you might follow, patiently carrying your own cross, and upon that, dying to yourself for Him. If we die with Him, we shall also live with Him. "If we are partakers of His sufferings, we shall also be partakers of His glory" (Romans 8:17).

Why do you seek another path to glory but that in which you are called to follow the "Captain of your salvation?" The life of Christ was a continual cross, and you desire a life of perpetual ease and joy?

You should know that your life must be a continual death to the appetites and passions of fallen nature. You should also know that the more perfectly you die to yourself, the more truly will you begin to live to God.

If you would enjoy true peace here and obtain the unfading crown of glory in the coming age, it is necessary that in every place and in all events you should willingly bear the cross. If you accept the call to follow Christ, part of your calling will be the call to suffer. To suffer patiently and willingly is the great testimony of your love and allegiance to your Lord.

Therefore prepare your spirit to suffer patiently the many inconveniences and troubles of this life. Plenty of these you will find, and you can never avoid them, even though you run to the ends of the earth or hide yourself in its deepest caverns. And only patient suffering can disarm their power or heal the wounds they have made.

As long as every tribulation is painful and grievous, and it is the desire of your soul to avoid it, you cannot be anything but miserable. What you work so hard to shun will follow you wherever you go. The patient enduring of the cross, and the death of self upon it, are the indispensable duties of fallen man. Only in this way can he be delivered from his darkness, corruption, and misery, and be restored to the possession of life, light, and peace.

If we have no other desire but that of ardently reaching after Him, of dwelling forever with Him, and of becoming nothing before Him, we should accept all of His dealings with us – whether obscurity or illumination, fruitfulness or barrenness, weakness or strength, sweetness or bitterness, temptations, wanderings, pain, weariness, or doubtings. And none of these things should slow our progress or alter our course.

10

On Mortification

All efforts to merely change the exterior thrust the soul yet farther outward into those things that it is so warmly and zealously battling. In this way, its powers are diffused and scattered abroad. Its energies and attentions are immediately directed to externals, thus it invigorates the very senses it is aiming to subdue.

This type of mortification can never subdue the passions or lessen their activity. The only method to accomplish this is inward silence. By this silence the soul is turned wholly and altogether inward to possess a present God.

If it directs all its vigour and energy toward this centre of its being, the simple act separates and withdraws it from the senses. The exercising of all its powers internally leaves the senses faint and powerless. The nearer the soul draws to God, the farther it is separated from the senses, and the less the passions are influenced by them.

In the mortification of the eye and ear, which continually supply the busy imagination with new subjects, there is little danger of falling into excess. God will teach us this, and we have only to follow where His Spirit guides.

The soul has a double advantage by proceeding in this way. In withdrawing from outward objects, it draws nearer to God. And the nearer its approaches are made to Him, besides the secret and sustaining power and virtue it receives, it is farther removed from sin. The result is that finally the state of having the mind turned to God becomes, as it were, habitual.

11

On Resignation

We should give up our whole existence unto God. This will come from the strong and positive conviction that while we are faithfully endeavouring to follow Him, the occurrence of every moment is agreeable to His immediate will and permission, and it is just what our present state requires. This conviction will make us resigned in all things, and we will accept all that happens, not as from this man or the other, but as from God Himself.

But I entreat you who sincerely wish to give yourselves up to God: After you have made the donation, do not snatch yourselves back again. Remember that a gift once presented is no longer at the disposal of the donor.

Resignation is a matter of the greatest importance in our progress. It is the key to the inner court. Whoever knows how to truly resign himself soon becomes pure and holy. We must, therefore, continue steadfast and immovable in this way, and not listen to the voice of natural reason. Great faith produces great resignation. We must confide in God, "hoping against hope" (Romans 4:18).

Resignation is casting off all selfish care, so that we may be completely at the disposal of God. All Christians are exhorted to resignation, for it is said, "Do not be anxious for tomorrow. Your heavenly Father knows all that you need" (Matthew 6:32,34). "In all your ways acknowledge Him, and He shall direct your paths" (Proverbs 3:6). "Commit your works to the Lord, and your thoughts will be established" (Proverbs 16:3). "Commit your way to the Lord; Trust also in Him, and He will bring it to pass. And He shall make your righteousness to go forth as the light, and your judgment as the noonday" (Psalm 37:5-6).

This virtue is practised by continually losing our own will in the will of God, by being resigned in all things. It is leaving what is past in oblivion, and what is to come, after having faithfully done our part, to the direction of God.

Resignation is devoting the present moment to Him by attributing nothing that we encounter to any other creature, but regarding all things in God; that is, to be looking upon all things, excepting only our sins, as infallibly proceeding from Him. Surrender yourselves then to be led and disposed of, just as God pleases.

We must willingly cooperate with, and affirm, the designs of God. These will tend to divest us of all our own plans so that in their place His purposes may be instituted. Let this be done in you and do not allow yourself to be attached to any thing, however good it may appear. It is no longer good if it in any measure turns you aside from that which God wills for you.

The Divine Will is preferable to everything else. It is our conformity to this sweet yoke that introduces us into the regions of internal peace. In this way we may know that the rebellion of our will is the chief occasion of all our disquiet. This is also the cause why we suffer so much uneasiness and anxiety.

Oh! If we did but submit our wills to the Divine will and to all its disposals, what tranquillity we would feel! What sweet peace! What inward serenity! What supreme delight and foretastes of blessedness! Let us shake off then all attachment to the interests of self and live on Faith and Resignation alone.

12

On Virtue

It is in this way that we acquire virtue with efficiency and certainty. For as God is the fountain and principle of all virtue, as we come closer to possessing Him, we will, to the same degree, rise into the most eminent virtues. Indeed, he that has God has all things, and he that does not have Him has nothing.

All virtue is but a mask, an outside appearance, changeable as our clothing, if it does not spring from this Divine source. But if it does, it is indeed genuine, essential, and permanent. "The King's daughter," says the psalmist, "is all glorious within" (Psalm 45:13).

13

On Conversion

"Turn! Turn from your evil ways! Why will you die, O house of Israel?" (Ezekiel 33:11). "Return to Him you have so greatly revolted against, O Israelites" (Isaiah 31:6). To be truly converted is to avert wholly from the creature and turn wholly unto God.

For the attainment of salvation, it is absolutely necessary that we should forsake outward sin and turn unto righteousness. However, this alone is not a perfect conversion, which consists in a total change of the whole man from an outward to an inward life.

When the soul is once turned to God, it finds a wonderful facility in continuing steadfast in its conversion. The longer it remains thus converted, the nearer it approaches, and the more firmly it adheres, to God. It thus follows, of necessity, that the nearer it draws to Him, the farther it is removed from that spirit which is contrary to Him. Therefore the soul is so effectively established and rooted in its conversion that a state of union becomes in some measure natural to it.

Now, we must not suppose that this is effected by a violent exertion of its own powers. The reason is that the soul is not capable of, nor should it attempt, any other cooperation with Divine Grace than that of endeavouring to withdraw itself from external objects and to turn inward. After this, it has nothing more to do than to continue steadfast in its adherence to God.

God has an attractive virtue which draws the soul more and more powerfully to Himself the nearer it comes to Him, and in attracting, He purifies and refines it.

It is the same as with a gross vapour exhaled by the sun which, as it gradually ascends, is rarified and rendered pure. The vapour, indeed, contributes to its exhalation only by its passiveness but the soul cooperates with the attractions of its God by a free and affectionate correspondence. This turning of the mind inward is both easy and efficacious, advancing the soul naturally and without constraint, because God Himself is the centre which attracts it.

All our care and attention should therefore be to acquire inward silence. Let us not be discouraged by the pains and difficulties we encounter in this exercise. They will soon be recompensed on the part of our God by such abundant supplies of His strength as will render the exercise perfectly easy. He will do this if we are faithful in meekly withdrawing our hearts from outward objects and gratifications, and returning to our centre, with affections full of tenderness and serenity.

When at any time the passions are turbulent, a gentle retreat inward unto a present God easily deadens and pacifies them. Any other way of contending with them rather irritates than appeases them. One word of our Saviour, in time past, instantly calmed a boisterous and raging sea. Can we now doubt, if we sincerely apply to Him in our distress, that He would still the tumults of the agitated soul?

14

On Self-Annihilation

The Soul becomes fitted for union with God by giving up Self to the destroying and annihilating power of Divine Love. This, indeed, is a most essential and necessary sacrifice in the Christian religion. It is in this way only that we pay true homage to the sovereignty of God.

By the destruction of the existence of Self within us, we truly acknowledge the supreme existence of our God. Unless we cease to exist in Self, the Spirit of the Eternal Word cannot exist in us. It is by the giving up of our own life that we make room for His coming. In dying to ourselves, He Himself lives and abides in us (Galatians 2:20).

We should, indeed, surrender our whole being unto Christ Jesus and cease to live any longer in ourselves. Only then may He Himself become our life, "that being dead, our life may be hid with Christ in God" (Colossians 3:3).

By leaving and forsaking ourselves, we are lost in Him. This can be effected only by the annihilation of Self. This is, in fact, the true prayer of adoration and renders unto "God and to the Lamb, blessing, and honour, and glory, and power for ever and ever!" (Revelation 5:13).

This is the Prayer of Truth. It is worshiping God "in spirit and in truth" (John 4:23). In this way we come to know the Spirit helping us in our infirmities and making intercession for us (Romans 8:26). Being influenced in this manner by the pure Spirit of God, we are drawn forth and freed from our own carnal and corrupt manner of praying.

We can pay due honour to God only in our own annihilation. This is no sooner accomplished than He fills us with Himself, because He never allows a void to remain anywhere.

If we only knew the virtues and blessings that the soul derives from this type of prayer, we would gladly be engaged in it without ceasing.

It is the pearl of great price (Matthew 13:44). It is the hidden treasure the man finds and freely sells all that he has in order to purchase it (Matthew 13:46). It is the "well of living water, springing up into everlasting life" (John 4:14). It is the true adoration of God. This life of prayer comprehends the full performance of the purest evangelical principles and precepts.

Jesus Christ assures us that the "Kingdom of God is within us" (Luke 17:21). This is true in two senses.

First, God becomes so fully the Master and Lord in us that nothing resists His dominion. Then He has established His Kingdom within us, in our interior.

Second, when we possess God, who is the supreme Good, we possess His kingdom also. This is the fulness of joy. It is here that we attain the end of our being created. The end of our creation, indeed, is to enjoy our God – even in this life.

But alas! How few ever come to know the pure joy which His Presence gives.

15

Man Acts More Nobly Under The Divine Influence Than He Can Possibly Do By Following His Own Will

When some people hear of the prayer of silence, they falsely imagine that the soul remains dead and inactive. However, the unquestionable truth is that, in this manner of prayer, it acts more nobly and more extensively than it has ever done before. For God Himself is its Mover, and it now acts by the agency of His Spirit.

When the apostle Paul speaks of our being led by the Spirit of God, it is not meant that we should cease from action. Instead, Paul means that we should act through the internal agency of His grace.

This is wonderfully represented by the prophet Ezekiel's vision of the wheels, which had a Living Spirit. Wherever the Spirit was to go, they went. They ascended and descended as they were moved. The Spirit of Life was in them, and they did not turn aside (Ezekiel 1:15-21).

In the same way, the soul should be subservient to the will of that animating Spirit that has enlightened it. It should be scrupulously faithful to follow only as that Spirit moves.

Our activity should, therefore, consist in endeavouring to acquire and maintain such a state as may be most open to Divine impressions and most flexible to all the operations of the Eternal Word.

As long as a canvas is unsteady, the painter is unable to produce a true copy. Even so, every act of our own selfish spirit is productive of false and erroneous images. It interrupts the work and defeats the design of this adorable Painter. Therefore, we must remain in peace and move only when He moves us. Jesus Christ has this Life in Himself (John 5:26), and He is the life of every living soul.

Since all action is worthy only in proportion to the dignity of the motivating principle, this action is incontestably more noble than any other. Actions produced by a Divine principle are Divine, but creaturely actions, however good they may appear, are merely human.

Jesus Christ, the Word, has the Life in Himself. Being communicative of His nature, He desires to communicate it to man. We should, therefore, make room for the influx of this Life. This can only be done by the ejection of the fallen nature and the suppression of the activity of Self.

This agrees with Paul's assertion: "If any man is in Christ, he is a new creature. Old things are passed away; behold, all things have become new!" (2 Corinthians 5:17). This state can be accomplished only by dying to ourselves and to all our own activity so that the influence of God may be substituted for the willful decisions of self.

Man may, indeed, open the window, but it is the Sun Himself that must give the Light. Jesus Christ has exemplified this in the Gospel. Martha did what was right, but because she did it in the power of her own spirit, Christ rebuked her.

The spirit of man is restless and turbulent. This is why it actually accomplishes little, though it appears to be doing much.

"Martha," said Christ, "You are worried and upset about many things, but only one thing is needed. Mary has chosen what is better, and it will not be taken away from her" (Luke 10:41-42).

What was it that Mary had chosen? Repose, tranquillity, and peace. She apparently ceased to act, so that the Spirit of Christ might act in her. She ceased to live, so that Christ might be her life.

The apostle Peter, in the warmth of his affection, told the Lord that, for His sake, he was ready and willing to lay down his life. But at the word of a young girl, he denied Him.

The many troubles in life are caused by the soul not abiding in its place and not being content with the will of God. These difficulties occur when we are not satisfied with what God gives from time to time.

Many people may be resigned to God's general will, but they fail in regard to the situation at the present moment. Being out of the will of God, they fall. They will continue in such falls as long as they continue out of the Divine will. When they return into it, all will go on well.

God loves what is done in His own order, and of His own will and time. While you faithfully give yourself up to His divine plan and purpose, you will do all things right.

All men have ardent desires – to a greater or lesser extent – except those who live in the Divine will. Some of these desires may appear to be good, but unless they are according to the will of God, they are out from self. These will only bring trouble and turmoil to the unsettled heart. He who rests in the circumstances of the Divine will, though he is exempt from all those desires, is infinitely more peaceful and glorifies God more.

This shows us how necessary it is to renounce ourselves and all our own activity so we may follow Jesus Christ. We cannot follow Him without being animated with His Spirit. In order for His Spirit to gain admission in us, it is necessary that our own spirit should first be subdued. "He that is joined to the Lord," says Paul, "is one spirit" (1 Corinthians 6:17).

All things should be done in their season. Every situation has its commencement, its progress, and its consummation. It is an unhappy error to stop in the beginning. Even the most artistic things have a natural process. At first we must labour with diligence and toil, but at last we shall reap the harvest of our industry.

When the vessel is in port, the mariners find it necessary to exert all their strength in order to guide her safely into the open sea. But once they are in the open waters, they are able to turn her with little effort, just as they please.

In the same way, while the soul remains in sin and fleshly entanglements, very frequent and strenuous efforts are required to bring it to a state of freedom. The cords that hold it must be loosed. After this loosing, by strong and vigorous efforts, it gradually pushes off from its old port. In leaving that port behind, it proceeds to the haven to which it wishes to travel.

When the vessel is put in motion in this way, she leaves the land behind in direct proportion to the distance she travels on the sea. The farther she travels from the old harbour, the less difficulty and labour is necessary in moving her forward. After a while, she begins to get the pleasant winds in her sails. She now proceeds so swiftly in her course that the oar, which has become useless, is laid aside.

How is the pilot now employed? He is content with spreading the sails and holding the rudder. To spread the sails is to lay the mind open before God that it may be acted upon by His Spirit. To hold the rudder is to restrain the heart from wandering from the true course – recalling it gently and guiding it steadily to the dictates of the blessed Spirit, which gradually gain possession and dominion of it. This occurs as the wind gradually fills the sails and propels the vessel.

While the winds are fair, the mariners rest from their labours. The vessel glides rapidly along without much effort on their part. When they rest in this way, and leave the vessel to the wind, they cover more distance in one hour than they had done in a much greater amount of time, with all their former efforts. If they were to try to use the oar now, they would not only tire themselves out, they would also slow the vessel by their ill-timed labours.

This is the manner of acting we should pursue internally. It will certainly advance us in a very short time, by His Divine influence, infinitely further than a whole life spent in repeated acts of self-exertion. Anyone who will take this path will find it much easier than any other.

If the wind becomes contrary and blows up a storm, instead of putting out to sea, we must cast anchor to hold the vessel. Our anchor is a firm confidence and hope in God. We wait patiently for the calming of the tempest and the return of more favourable winds, just as David "waited patiently for the Lord, and He turned to him and heard his cry" (Psalm 40:1).

We must, therefore, be resigned to the Spirit of God. We must give ourselves wholly to His divine guidance, never allowing ourselves to be disturbed by any accident. A sense of unrest is the door by which the enemy gets into the soul to rob it of its peace. In the same way, we should not busy ourselves with what others say or do, because this will also be a great cause of disturbance to us.

Let us calm all the motions of our heart, as soon as we sense it is in agitation. Let us stop all pleasure that comes from any source other than God alone. Let us get rid of all unprofitable thoughts or meditations. Let us diligently seek God within us. We shall undoubtedly find Him, and with Him, joy and peace.

This joy and peace are of such a quality that they will endure in the midst of suffering. Because they flow from an inexhaustible source, they become a perpetual fountain of delight. "Peace I leave with you," said Christ to His followers, "my peace I give to you, not as the world gives; my peace I give to you" (John 14:27).

If we only knew the blessing that comes from listening and responding to the voice of God, and how greatly the soul is strengthened and invigorated by this practice, all flesh would surely be silent before the Lord (Zechariah 2:13). All would be still as soon as He appears.

To draw us further into a total surrender to Him, God assures us that we should fear nothing in giving ourselves completely to Him. He takes care of us in a way that far surpasses the highest tenderness that we could even imagine or conceive. "Can a woman," He says, "forget the child at her breast and have no compassion on the child she has borne? Though she may forget, yet I will not forget you" (Isaiah 49:15).

Oh blessed assurance, full of comfort and consolation! Who, after this, could be fearful of fully resigning themselves to the provision and guidance of their God!

All men search for peace, but they look where it is not to be found. They seek it in the world that is continuously promising, but can never give, solid peace. The problem is this: Wherever we go, we will carry this fruitful source of every perplexity and difficulty – our own unsubdued and selfish will. The love of liberty is one of the most dangerous passions of the heart. If we follow this fleshly tendency, instead of giving true liberty, it reduces us to slavery.

Since our passions are the worst of our tyrants, if we obey them even partially, we will insure that we are always in perpetual strife and conflict within. If we choose to give ourselves up entirely to them, it is horrid to think of the excesses to which they may lead. They will torment the heart. Like a torrent, they will sweep all before them, and yet never be satisfied.

True liberty is found only in Him whose truth shall set us free (John 8:32). As we follow His ways, we shall experience the reality that to serve Him is to reign.

That holiness by which we are sanctified and entirely devoted to God consists in precisely doing His will in every circumstance of life. Take what steps you please, do what deeds you will, let them shine with the brightest lustre, yet you will not be rewarded unless you have done the will of your Sovereign Master.

Although your servant did wonderful things in your house, if he did not do what you asked of him, you would not value his service. You might even complain of him as a bad servant, and have reason to do so.

There is no good spirit but the Spirit of God. Any spirit that removes us from the true good is only a spirit of illusion, no matter how flattering it may appear. Who would want to be carried in a magnificent chariot on the road to an abyss?! The path to a deep precipice is dangerous and frightening, even if it is covered with roses. The way that leads to a crown is delightful, even though it may be thickly covered with thorns.

He has given us His good Spirit to instruct us (Nehemiah 9:20). Therefore let us no longer follow our own will but only follow His. Then not only our religious actions but also all our activities will be done with no other purpose than that of pleasing Him. Then will our whole conduct be sanctified. Then will our deeds become a continual sacrifice. Incessant prayer and uninterrupted love will occupy the heart.

Let us, therefore, submit to the annihilation of our own will so that He may reign in us! For it is His prerogative to command and our duty to obey.

16

On The Possession Of Peace And Rest Before God

The soul that is faithful in the exercise of that love and adherence to God which has been already described is astonished to feel Him gradually taking possession of its whole being. That same soul now enjoys a continual sense of that presence which has become, as it were, natural to it.

This presence diffuses an unusual serenity throughout all our faculties – it calms the mind and gives sweet repose and quiet, even in the midst of our daily labours. However, for this to become continuous, we must be resigned to Him without reserve.

We must, however, urge the soul, as a matter of the highest importance, to cease from self-action and self-exertion so that God Himself may act alone. He says by the mouth of His prophet David, "Be still and know that I am God" (Psalm 46:10).

Those who accuse this kind of prayer as being nothing more than a form of idleness are greatly mistaken. Such a charge can arise only from spiritual inexperience. If they would only make some attempt at attaining this method of prayer, they would soon experience the complete opposite of what they suppose, and they will find their accusations to be groundless.

This appearance of inactivity is, indeed, not the consequence of sterility and emptiness but of fruitfulness and abundance. This will be clearly perceived by the experienced soul. This soul will know and feel that its silence is full of vitality. This is the result of causes that are totally the reverse of apathy and barrenness.

The interior is not a stronghold to be taken by storm and violence. It is a kingdom of Peace that is to be gained only by Love. Let us then give ourselves up to God without apprehension of danger. He will love us and enable us to love Him. That love, increasing daily, will produce all other virtues in us. He alone is able to replenish our hearts which the world has agitated and intoxicated but never been able to fill.

He will not take anything from us except those things that make us unhappy. He will only make us despise the world, which perhaps we do already. We will need to alter our actions a little, and we will need to correct the motive for them by making everything referable to Him. Then the most ordinary and seemingly indifferent actions will become exercises of virtue and sources of consolation.

We shall even behold the approach of death in peace; we will see it as the beginning of immortality. As Paul says, "We shall not be unclothed but clothed, and mortality shall be swallowed up by life" (2 Corinthians 5:4).

Let us, therefore, no longer be afraid to commit ourselves wholly to God. What risk do we run in depending solely on Him?! Ah! He will not deceive us, unless He gives us an abundance far beyond our highest hopes. But those who expect to receive all from themselves will inevitably be deceived. They will have to suffer this rebuke of God by His prophet Isaiah: "Behold all you that kindle a fire and provide yourselves with flaming torches, walk in the light of your fire and in the torches you have set ablaze. This is what you receive from my hand: You will lie down in sorrow" (Isaiah 50:11).

The soul that has advanced this far has no need of any other preparation than its state of rest. Now the Presence of God, which is the great effect, through the continual state of prayer, begins to be powerfully felt. The soul experiences what the Apostle Paul declares, that "Eye has not seen, ear has not heard, neither has it entered into the heart of man, the things that God has prepared for those that love Him" (1 Corinthians 2:9).

The soul certainly feels transcendent blessedness and feels that it is no longer "I that live but Christ that lives in me" (Galatians 2:20). We come to realise that the only way to find Christ and abide in Him is to turn from all external things and seek Him with all our heart. We no sooner do this than we are filled with the consolations and blessings of His Presence. We are amazed at such a wonderful blessing, and we begin to experience internal communion that external matters cannot interrupt.

The same thing may be said of this type of prayer that is said of wisdom: "All good things come together with her." For virtue now flows from us and is transformed into action with so much sweetness and ease that they appear natural and spontaneous.

17

On Perfection, or The Union Of The Soul With God

The most profitable and desirable state in this life is that of Christian perfection. This perfection consists in the union of the soul with God, a union that includes in it all spiritual good. It produces in us a wonderful freedom of spirit which raises us above all the events and changes of this life, and that frees us from the tyranny of human fear. It gives us an extraordinary power for doing every task that lies before us, and for sufficiently fulfilling every commitment. From this union, we receive a true Christian prudence in all our undertakings and a peace and perfect tranquillity in every condition and circumstance. In short, it is a continual victory over self-love and all our passions.

It is impossible to attain Divine Union solely by the activity of meditation, or by the softening of the affections, or even by the highest degree of enlightened and elegantly composed prayer. According to Scripture, "no man shall see God and live" (Exodus 33:20). So even if we practice conversational prayer and are in a state of active contemplation, if it is being performed in the *life* and *strength* of our own will, we "cannot in this way see God." Everything that is of man's own power and exertion – no matter how noble or highly exalted it may be – must first die.

In his vision of the Revelation of Jesus Christ, John relates "that there was silence in heaven" (Revelation 8:1). Now heaven represents the centre of the soul where, before the majesty of God appears, all must be hushed to silence. All the efforts, even the very existence, of Self-love must be destroyed, because it is the natural will of man that is opposed to God. All the malignity of man proceeds from it, so it is a reality that the purity of the soul increases in direct proportion to the natural will becoming subjected to the Divine Will.

This is the reason that the soul can never arrive at Divine Union by any way other than the annihilation of its own will. Nor can it ever become one with God but by being re-established in the purity of its first creation.

God purifies the soul by His Wisdom, as refiners purify metals in the furnace. Gold can only be purified by fire, which gradually separates out all that is earthly and impure and consumes it. The gold must be melted and dissolved and all impure mixtures taken away by casting it again and again into the furnace. In this way it is refined from all internal corruption, and even exalted to a state that is incapable of further purification. It no longer contains any adulterous mixture; its purity is perfect, and its simplicity complete. It is fit for the most exquisite workmanship.

So we are able to see that the Divine Spirit, as an unremitting fire, must devour and destroy all self-activity and all that is earthly, sensual, and carnal before the soul can be fitted for, and capable of, union with God.

"I will make a man more precious than fine gold" (Isaiah 13:12). When God begins to burn, destroy, and purify, then the soul, not perceiving the healthy purposes of these operations, shrinks from them. As the gold seems to blacken rather than brighten when first put into the furnace, so the soul conceives that its purity is lost, and that its temptations are sins.

We gladly confess that the enjoyment of God is the end for which we were created, that "without holiness" (Hebrews 12:14) none can attain it, and that to attain it, we must necessarily pass through a severe and purifying process. With that understanding, it is strange that we should dread and avoid this process, as if it could be the cause of evil and imperfection in this present life which is to be productive of glory and blessedness in the life to come!

Let us all, then, press forward toward the mark, allowing ourselves to be guided and governed by the Spirit of Grace, which will infallibly conduct us to the ultimate end of our creation, which is the enjoyment of God.

Perhaps it may be said that some may pretend to have attained this blessed state. Alas! None can any more fake this than the wretch who, on the point of perishing with hunger, is able for an extended time to make the appearance of being full and satisfied. Some wish or word, some sigh or sign, will inevitably escape him and betray his famished state.

"Be perfect, even as your Father in heaven is perfect" (Matthew 5:48). The soul that remains in its disorderly will is imperfect. It becomes more perfect as it approaches nearer to the will of God. When a soul is advanced so far that it cannot, in anything, depart from the Divine will, it then becomes wholly perfect – united with and transformed into the Divine nature. Being thus purified and united to God, it finds a profound peace and a sweet rest which brings it to such a perfect union of love that it is filled with joy. It conforms itself to the will of its God in all emergencies and rejoices to do the Divine good pleasure in every situation.

The Lord draws near to such a soul and communicates Himself inwardly to it. He fills it with Himself, because it is empty. He clothes it with His light and with His love, because it is naked. He lifts it up, because it is low, and He unites it with Himself.

If you would enter into this heaven on earth, forget every care and every anxious thought. Get out of yourself so that the love of God may live in your soul. Then you may be enabled to say with the Apostle, "I live, yet not I, but Christ lives in me" (Galatians 2:20).

How happy we would be if we could leave all for God and seek Him only, if we could breathe after none but Him, and let only Him have our sighs! Oh, if only we could go on without interruption toward this blessed state!

God calls us to it. He invites us to make Him our inward centre so that He can renew us and change us. Here He will show us a new and heavenly kingdom, full of joy, peace, contentment, and serenity.

The spiritual and abiding soul no longer has its peace broken. It may encounter fierce battles. The prince of darkness may indeed make violent assaults against it, but the restful soul stands firm against them, like a strong pillar. It may sometimes be naked, forsaken, opposed, and desolate, but the tempests never reach to that serene heaven within where pure and perfect love resides. Nothing more happens to it than happens to a high mountain in a storm.

The valley is darkened with thick clouds, fierce tempests of hail, and thunder. The lofty mountain glitters by the bright beams of the sun, in quietness and serenity, continuing clear like heaven – immovable and full of light. Such a soul is indeed like "Mount Zion, which cannot be moved but endures forever" (Psalm 125:1).

In this throne of quiet, the perfections of spiritual beauty are manifested. Here we shall enjoy the true light of the secret and divine mysteries of Christ – perfect humility, the amplest resignation, the meekness and innocence of the dove, liberty and purity of heart. Here we see joyful simplicity, heavenly indifference, continual prayer, a total transparency, perfect disinterest in earthly things, and a life of heavenly thought and conversation.

This is the rich and hidden treasure. This is the pearl of great price.

Buy online at our website: **www.KingsleyPress.com**
This book is also available as an eBook for Kindle,
Nook and iBooks.

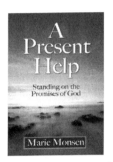

An Ordered Life

An Autobiography by G. H. Lang

G. H. Lang was a remarkable Bible teacher, preacher and writer of a past generation who should not be forgotten by today's Christians. He inherited the spiritual "mantle" of such giants in the faith as George Müller, Anthony Norris Groves and other notable saints among the early Brethren movement. He traveled all over the world with no fixed means of support other than prayer and faith and no church or other organization to depend on. Like Mr. Müller before him, he told his needs to no one but God. Many times his faith was tried to the limit, as funds for the next part of his journey arrived only at the last minute and from unexpected sources.

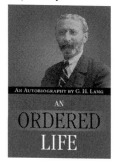

This autobiography traces in precise detail the dealings of God with his soul, from the day of his conversion at the tender age of seven, through the twilight years when bodily infirmity restricted most of his former activities. You will be amazed, as you read these pages, to see how quickly and continually a soul can grow in grace and in the knowledge of spiritual things if they will wholly follow the Lord.

Horace Bushnell once wrote that every man's life is a plan of God, and that it's our duty as human beings to find and follow that plan. As Mr. Lang looks back over his long and varied life in the pages of this book, he frequently points out the many times God prepared him in the present for some future work or role. Spiritual life applications abound throughout the book, making it not just a life story but a spiritual training manual of sorts. Preachers will find sermon starters and illustrations in every chapter. Readers of all kinds will benefit from this close-up view of the dealings of God with the soul of one who made it his life's business to follow the Lamb wherever He should lead.

Buy online at our website: **www.KingsleyPress.com**
Also available as an eBook for Kindle, Nook and iBooks.

THE AWAKENING
By Marie Monsen

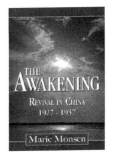

REVIVAL! It was a long time coming. For twenty long years Marie Monsen prayed for revival in China. She had heard reports of how God's Spirit was being poured out in abundance in other countries, particularly in nearby Korea; so she began praying for funds to be able to travel there in order to bring back some of the glowing coals to her own mission field. But that was not God's way. The still, small voice of God seemed to whisper, "What is happening in Korea can happen in China if you will pay the price in prayer." Marie Monsen took up the challenge and gave her solemn promise: "Then I will pray until I receive."

The Awakening is Miss Monsen's own vivid account of the revival that came in answer to prayer. Leslie Lyall calls her the "pioneer" of the revival movement—the handmaiden upon whom the Spirit was first poured out. He writes: "Her surgical skill in exposing the sins hidden within the Church and lurking behind the smiling exterior of many a trusted Christian—even many a trusted Christian leader—and her quiet insistence on a clear-cut experience of the new birth set the pattern for others to follow."

The emphasis in these pages is on the place given to prayer both before and during the revival, as well as on the necessity of self-emptying, confession, and repentance in order to make way for the infilling of the Spirit.

One of the best ways to stir ourselves up to pray for revival in our own generation is to read the accounts of past awakenings, such as those found in the pages of this book. Surely God is looking for those in every generation who will solemnly take up the challenge and say, with Marie Monsen, "I will pray until I receive."

Buy online at our website: **www.KingsleyPress.com**
Also available as an eBook for Kindle, Nook and iBooks.

Printed in Great Britain
by Amazon